ON THE TEAM

GYMNASTICS

By Kathy Meyer

Gareth Stevens
Publishing

Please visit our website, www.garethstevens.com. For a free color catalog of all our high-quality books, call toll free 1-800-542-2595 or fax 1-877-542-2596.

Library of Congress Cataloging-in-Publication Data

Meyer, Kathy.
Gymnastics / Kathy Meyer.
     p. cm. — (On the team)
Includes index.
ISBN 978-1-4339-6446-6 (pbk.)
ISBN 978-1-4339-6447-3 (6-pack)
ISBN 978-1-4339-6444-2 (library binding)
1. Gymnastics—Juvenile literature. I. Title.
GV461.3.M49 2012
796.44—dc23
                                          2011032138

First Edition

Published in 2012 by
Gareth Stevens Publishing
111 East 14th Street, Suite 349
New York, NY 10003

Copyright © 2012 Gareth Stevens Publishing

Designer: Michael J. Flynn
Editor: Greg Roza

Photo credits: Cover, pp. 1, 8–9, 10, 17, 20, 21 Shutterstock.com; p. 5 iStockphoto.com; p. 6 Topical Press Agency/Hulton Archive/Getty Images; p. 13 Alistair Berg/Stone+/Getty Images; pp. 14, 15 by N-Focus Photography; p. 18 Franck Fife/AFP/Getty Images.

Printed in the United States of America

CPSIA compliance information: Batch #CW12GS: For further information contact Gareth Stevens, New York, New York at 1-800-542-2595.

Contents

Words in the glossary appear in **bold** type the first time they are used in the text.

Tumble with the Team!

Gymnastics is a great way to stay healthy. Young gymnasts start with **tumbling**. As they grow, they take part in harder events. The best gymnasts **compete** against **athletes** from other countries!

During a gymnastic competition, several events are held at the same time. However, the gymnasts take turns **performing** in an event one at a time. Each gymnast's score affects how the team as a whole does. Gymnasts practice together to help the team do well.

THE COACH'S CORNER

There are a few different kinds of gymnastics. This book is about the kind called artistic gymnastics.

Many gymnasts begin training when they're very young.

Olympic gymnastics briefly included three events in which teammates performed in time with each other. Judges graded the teams on things like difficulty and skill.

A gymnast from Denmark performs on the balance beam during the 1908 Olympics in London, England.

6

The History of Gymnastics

Gymnastics has been around for thousands of years. The ancient Greeks and Romans started some events that are still practiced today. Other ancient gymnastic events—such as swimming, wrestling, and jumping—are no longer considered gymnastics.

Modern gymnastics started in Europe during the late 1700s. It was used to help people stay healthy and to train soldiers. Competitive gymnastics became more popular with the first modern **Olympic Games** in 1896. The events—which included rope climbing and rock lifting—have changed a lot since then.

Power!

Gymnasts must be very strong to make it through an entire event without tiring. The strength to do something for a long time without getting tired is called endurance.

Male gymnasts compete in an event called the rings. They grab two hanging rings and hold themselves off the ground. Then they do a series of movements while holding the rings. These movements include flips, swings, and holds. Holds are very hard and take a lot of strength and endurance.

THE COACH'S CORNER

Gymnasts practice a routine for each event. A routine is a set of moves done in a certain order every time.

The rings are sometimes called still rings. That's because the rings aren't supposed to move much as a gymnast swings from one hold to another.

9

Gymnasts practice on beams that are only a few inches off the ground. During a competition, the beam is 4 feet (1.2 m) off the floor!

THE COACH'S CORNER

A gymnast ends a routine on the balance beam by performing a jump or flip to return to the floor. This is called a dismount.

On the Beam

Gymnasts must be flexible. That means they can bend easily without getting hurt. They must have finesse. That means their movements look smooth and skillful. They must have good balance, too.

Female gymnasts compete on the balance beam. Athletes jump onto a beam that's just 4 inches (10 cm) wide! They perform a routine that includes jumps, flips, and tumbling. Balance beam routines also include dance movements. The best balance beam gymnasts display balance, flexibility, and finesse during a routine.

Men's Gymnastics

Most gymnastic events for men focus on strength and endurance, but these athletes must also have good balance, flexibility, and finesse. The pommel horse was first made to help soldiers practice getting on and off horses. Today, male gymnasts perform routines on them using only their hands to touch the horse.

Men perform on two types of bars, too. The even bars are two bars placed next to each other. The high bar is a single bar. Bar routines include holds, swings, flips, and dismounts.

THE COACH'S CORNER

Both men and women perform in an event called the vault. Athletes jump off a springboard and push off a special table, then perform flips in the air.

During a pommel horse routine, gymnasts swing their legs in circular motions and use their hands to move across the horse.

13

The floor exercise can last up to 90 seconds. During that time, the gymnast does many "saltos," or flips.

THE COACH'S CORNER

Men also compete in the floor exercise. However, their routines don't include music or dance elements.

Women's Gymnastics

Women's events focus on strength, balance, and finesse. They perform routines on a set of bars at different heights called uneven bars. The routines include swings, flips, holds, and dismounts.

One of the most popular women's events is the floor exercise. This event doesn't require an **apparatus**. Gymnasts perform on a mat that is 40 by 40 feet (12 by 12 m). Routines are performed to music and include a mixture of tumbling and dance skills. The gymnasts often look like ballet dancers!

At the Meet

Gymnastic teams must practice very hard to become stronger and learn routines. Their goal is to win **medals** at a gymnastic competition, or meet.

There are two types of meets during a year. The first is the compulsory season. "Compulsory" means required. Every gymnast must perform the same routines on all the apparatuses. Teams with the highest scores win medals. The other competition is the optional season. "Optional" means by choice. Gymnasts can perform their own routines during the optional season.

Gymnastic meets are organized by age and level of ability. That way, gymnasts at lower levels can win medals, too.

Although they're not considered apparatuses, pads are very important to gymnastics. They keep the athletes from getting injured.

17

18

The number of top scores per team
that judges use for team scores
depends on the size of the meet
and the number of gymnasts.

What's the Score?

Before performing events, gymnasts start with "perfect scores." This might be a 10. During routines, judges take points away for mistakes. They also take points away if a gymnast's routine isn't as hard as others at the same level.

After every gymnast has performed every event, judges report which athletes have the best scores. The top gymnasts in each event win medals. Judges also give team medals. They add up each team's top scores and give medals for the highest scores.

THE COACH'S CORNER

The all-around winner is the gymnast who gets the highest overall score in all the events. It's the honor most gymnasts want to win.

At the Olympics

Gymnastics is a lot of hard work. Gymnasts must be in perfect **physical** health to win medals at meets. Teams work many hours together to make sure they have what it takes to get the highest scores.

Today, an Olympic medal is a gymnast's greatest honor. It takes years of practice to make it that far! Athletes from all over the world meet once every 4 years to compete in the Olympics. The best gymnasts win medals for their teams and countries.

Gymnastic Events

event	men/women	apparatus
balance beam	women	padded wooden or metal beam on metal legs
even bars	men	2 wooden bars of same height on metal frame
floor exercise	both	none
high bar	men	steel bar on metal frame supported by cables
pommel horse	men	padded "horse" with wooden or plastic "pommels," or handles, supported by metal legs
rings	men	two metal or wooden rings attached to straps, supported by metal frame and cables
uneven bars	women	2 wooden bars of different heights, supported by metal frame and cables
vault	both	a springboard to jump from and a padded table to push against

Glossary

apparatus: a tool or object needed to perform in a gymnastic event

athlete: someone who is physically fit and competes in sporting events

compete: to try to do better than others who are doing the same thing

medal: a prize given to the winners of a competition. They are often made of metal and worn on a ribbon around the neck.

Olympic Games: an international sports competition held once every 2 years, switching back and forth between summer and winter games

perform: to carry out an action

physical: having to do with the body

tumbling: simple gymnastic exercises, such as jumps and rolls

For More Information

Books

Bray-Moffatt, Naia. *I Love Gymnastics*. New York, NY: DK Publishing, 2005.

Brown, Heather. *How to Improve at Gymnastics*. New York, NY: Crabtree Publishing, 2009.

Olsen, Leigh. *Going for Gold: The 2008 U.S. Women's Gymnastics Team*. New York, NY: Price Stern Sloan, 2008.

Websites

Artistic Gymnastics

www.olympic.org/artistic-gymnastics

Read about Olympic artistic gymnastic events, apparatuses, past medal winners, and much more.

USA Gymnastics

www.usa-gymnastics.org/pages/

Read about the US gymnastic team and find out how it ranks compared to international teams.

Index